WHERE THE WIND CIRCLES BACK

By Rabiya Nizam

Publisher

Power In Me Foundation

ISBN Paperback: 978-93-94749-38-2
ISBN Ebook: 978-93-94749-47-4

Publisher
Power In Me Foundation, H.No. 531, MIG-21, Near Subhadra Memorial Hospital, Opp. SBI Colony, Ganiyari Road, Waidhan, District- Singrauli, Madhya Pradesh-486886. Email id: mpowerinme@gmail.com, Mobile: 8851537816

Acknowledgement

This collection would not have been possible if not for the people and events that helped shape me as a person and as a creator. Life has been my greatest teacher—every joy, wound, and silence of experience has branched into a story to be written down. I owe an immense debt of gratitude to those whose inspiration or companionship propelled me beyond my limitations, as well as those who simply believed I could express my feelings creatively. To my friends, mentors, and readers who noticed meaning in my words, thank you for your belief in me, and for your warmth. I want to take a moment to send a hearty thank you to Manoj Sir, whose continuous guidance, encouragement, and wisdom has been my beacon of light in my fog of uncertainty. He has always pushed me to strive onward, to continue my creations, and to find meaning even among nonsense. His belief in my capacity to be expressive has helped me to be brave enough to own my voice and not only be an artist, but to continue pursuing opportunities without self-doubt.

Preface

This compilation of thirty poems is my travel through the human experience and the range of emotions it elicits. Each poem is a snapshot of a moment in life — the chilly breaths of horror, the gentle touch of love, the injuries of betrayal, the flames of sisterhood, and the biting truths of political satire. Together, they create an intermingling of thought and feeling that fits just as easily into darkness as it does to hope. I have not only engaged in expression but engaged in understanding — in meeting fear, in reveling in strength, and in examining the world we live in. Writing them developed into both a confrontation and a release, and it was a way to change my emotional narratives into writing that might resonate with others. Each poem is a little piece of my truth, a brief glimpse of the world as I have seen and felt it. Ultimately, this book is an offering from me to you, from my heart to yours.

TABLE OF CONTENT

1. The Moor Remembers

Through my eyes, the world is a wound— it bleeds sorrow into the grass, stains the air with the taste of rust.

I walk the moor at dusk, where stones lean like drunks in the fog, and the earth swallows footsteps whole. I came here for answers. Instead, I found her.

They say she loved too much, gave every smile away until there was nothing left to wear on her own face. Her happiness, her grief— all of it borrowed from others, and when they left, she was left hollow.

They say she buried her name somewhere out here. Some claim she burned it in the cremation pit behind the chapel, watching the flames lick away every reason to stay alive.

The wind here does not travel straight. It circles back, carrying questions in a voice almost like mine: "Do you love me? Am I enough?" Nher. No one ever answers me.

I think I am walking the path she took. The grass remembers the weight of her knees, the stones remember her hands pressed to their cold faces, begging for someone to stay. And I— I feel my heart loosening, dropping threads into the soil as I go.

When the mist comes down from the hill, I can't tell if my skin is mine or hers. The air tastes like ash. My voice sounds older than my years. And in the pause between each breath, I feel her smile stretching inside my own.

They will tell stories of me one day— the woman who waits where the earth swallows sound, asking strangers in the fog, "Do you love me?" And when they answer yes, I will take the warmth from their chests, leaving them sleeping in the grass.

Through my eyes, the world has become a beautiful, painful place. And I am not sure anymore if I am living or simply haunting.

LOVE
LOVE
LOVE
LOVE
LOVE

2. Between Your Words And My Silence

I think we should take a step back—
not to run away,
but to breathe without choking
on the weight of what we never say.

You tell me you love me,
but that love hides
like sunlight behind thick clouds—
present, yet never warming my skin.

We never seem to have
a conversation
that walks without stumbling.
You see me as overbearing,
I see you as locked away,
a door I keep knocking on,
knuckles sore from the effort.

You say you love me—
but I cannot feel it
in the spaces between your actions.
Sometimes,
you pull me close
like you cannot imagine life without me.
Other times,
you turn to ice,

cold enough to make me doubt
if your hands were ever warm.

And trust?
It slips through my fingers
like water that was never mine to hold.

I wanted to speak these words
while looking into your eyes,
but you rarely look up—
your gaze tethered to your work,
even when I am right there beside you.

So let us both
step away from this
and think.
Not to punish,
not to abandon,
but to see if love
still lives between your words
and my silence.

3. From Friendship's Shore To Love Horizon's

From laughter shared and late-night calls,
To moments where the silence falls,
We never guessed where this would go,
A spark grew soft, then bold, then glowed.

In comfort's gaze and steady hand,
We found a love we hadn't planned.
No grand confession, no clear start—
Just quiet beats of a growing heart.

Through seasons' change, both sun and rain,
We held the joy, we soothed the pain.
No need for masks, no need to hide,
You saw my soul from deep inside.

The way you listen, calm and true,
The way my thoughts lean close to you—
It felt like home, a place I knew,
Yet somehow shining, strange, and new.

Our laughter spilled through crowded streets,
Our shadows danced where twilight meets.
With every step, the line grew thin
Between where friends end, love begins.

No sudden blaze, no crashing wave,
But steady tides our courage gave.
And hand in hand, we came to see,
Love blooms in quiet mystery.

So here we stand, hearts open wide,
No map to keep, no rules to guide.
From friendship's shore, through skies above,
We sail toward the horizon of love.

YET I SAID YES

4. Yet I Said Yes

Though I may choose thee, still thy steps shall go,
For will's own law outstrips the chain of choice;
And I, left trembling in thy parting's throe,
Hear silent thunder in thy absent voice.

Farewells are daggers—yet the world moves on,
And all must walk beneath its ruthless sun;
Each trial leaves me bleeding, hope undone,
Each joy I grasp dissolves, as shadows run.

Yet in the wreckage, torn by grief's command,
With roses turned to thorns within my breast,
I find no healing—yet I choose to stand,
To greet the tempest as an honoured guest.

For though life rends the heart, and peace denies,
Still "Yes" I breathe beneath unpitying skies.

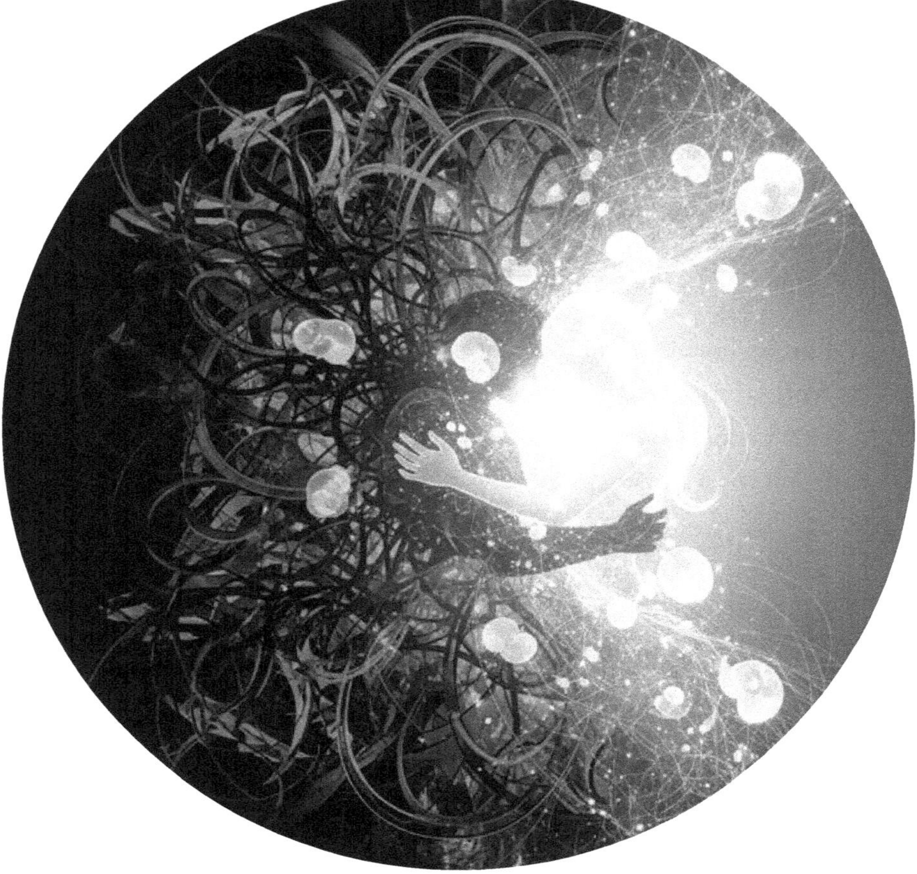

5. True Companions

It seems long past since first I chanced to find
The souls whose hearts beat steady next to mine;
For I was wandering, restless, deaf, and blind,
And sought for light where none was meant to shine.

I searched in places cold and far from home,
Through fleeting faces, voices strange and brief;
In every crowd I felt the urge to roam,
Yet found no balm to soothe my silent grief.

But all the while, unseen yet ever near,
They stood beside me, steadfast through the night;
And when my heart grew still enough to hear,
Their voices turned my darkness into light.

Now blessed I walk, for fortune led me true,
To friends whose love makes every sky seem blue.

6. Our Love Language

For the longest time, I've known your face,
Watch you grow in your own bright grace.
My baby girl—though grown today,
Still in my heart, you'll always stay.

You'll argue with me, just because you can—
It's your sweet, stubborn, lifelong plan.
If I say "blue," you'll laugh and say,
"It's pink! It's purple! Not your way."

Perhaps this is how our hearts converse,
A gentle spar in a playful verse;
A push, a pull, a knowing smile,
That makes the journey all worthwhile.

One day our roads will twist apart,
Yet you will live inside my heart;
At every turn, through joy or strife,
You'll find me walking in your life.

Forever yours, no matter where—
My love, my pride, my tender care.

7. Looking For My Missing Pieces

At this moment, I am about to flop spectacularly at the noble art of making sense. My brain is in shambles— not the cute kind of messy, like a kitchen after baking cookies, but the epic disaster kind, where the smoke alarm is having a full-blown opera solo and even the fire extinguisher is side-eyeing me.

Inside my skull, everything is a jigsaw puzzle with missing pieces— and not just missing, but stolen by some cosmic raccoon who's now running off into the void, cackling.

I try to gather my thoughts, but they scatter like children who just heard the ice cream truck. I call them back. They wave at me from somewhere three galaxies away.

So here I am, desperately hunting for a slice of sanity, a crumb, a half-melted ice cube of clarity from someone else's mind— because mine is playing hide and seek, and the "seek" part? I'm losing.

Oh, the irony— me, the one who always has something to say, now standing here with words like slippery fish sliding right through my hands. I reach for them, they wriggle away, leaving only scales of half-formed ideas that glitter but refuse to assemble.

Still, I speak. Or maybe I don't. Maybe I just gesture wildly like a tourist trying to explain "urgent bathroom" in a language they don't know. You look at me and tilt your head the way one does when trying to decode the shrieks of a distant bird.

Part of me wants to laugh at this— to roll in the absurdity, to crown myself Queen of the Unfinished Sentence. The other part aches, quietly, because buried under the comedy is the truth: sometimes I cannot find the path back to myself.

And maybe that's why I'm here, in front of you, hoping you'll hand me a compass made of kindness, or at least point to where my runaway thoughts are hiding.

If you do, I promise to return them in better shape. I'll feed them tea. I'll make them sit still. I'll write them into something that matters— a poem, a love letter, a note that says "I was lost, but I'm back now, and thank you for waiting."

8. Degrees In Dust

We build our towers of paper and ink,
scrolls wrapped in ribbons, names in gold,
parading across stages as though the tassel
were a halo.
We call it progress.

But the ink dries faster than our minds awaken.
We graduate into cubicles,
shackled to the same rusted chains
our ancestors dragged behind them—
prejudice polished to look like tradition,
hatred folded neatly into patriotism,
and ignorance dressed in academic robes.

Our books taught us history,
yet we still divide the living by the dead—
their grudges, their borders,
their sacred lines drawn in sand and blood.
We can calculate interest rates,
but not the interest in another's pain.
We can code in seven languages,
but cannot speak in kindness.

The degrees hang straight on our crooked walls,
proof not of wisdom,
but of a transaction—
tuition in, certificate out,
hands shaken, photographs taken,

souls untouched.

And so the educated keep their knives sharp,
not for carving knowledge,
but for carving neighbors.
The communal fires burn bright—
illuminating our diplomas,
but never our conscience.

We built universities to enlighten,
yet leave their gates with our minds
still flickering in the dark,
huddled around the embers
of old hatreds,
proudly calling it
heritage.

9. To My Mother Though Apart

Though scarce my mind recalls thy gentle face,
Nor keeps the record of thy voice's tone,
Yet in my heart thou hast a steadfast place,
A quiet shrine I claim as all thine own.

Without thy watch, I learned my tender years,
By other hands upheld through joy and pain;
They soothed my griefs, they calmed my childish fears,
And guided me to where my steps remain.

Yet oft, when dusk enfolds the silent sky,
And dreams awaken all that day forgets,
I bless thee still, for life's first gift was thy—
The light thou gav'st my soul forever debts.

Though time and distance keep our paths apart,
Thou hold'st, unlost, one chamber of my heart.

10. Truth and Thunder

I am **not** your glossy magazine cover.
Not the mannequin in a glass box
wearing empowerment like it's **on sale this season.**
I am **not** your cocktail glass,
perched on a rooftop bar,
pretending the skyline is freedom.
I am **not** your corporate badge
dangling from my neck
like proof I earned my existence.
I am not a **trend.**
I am not your **campaign.**
I am a living, thinking, breathing human—
with my own mind,
my own voice,
my own damn definition of modernity.

Somewhere along the way,
They sold us a costume and called it progress.
Sexy—but not threatening.
Confident—but not loud.
Smart—but never confrontational.
It's like they want us to roar—
but only in a whisper.
Well—
I'm done playing their balance beam game.
I stepped off.
I stepped into the storm.

Modernity isn't a hemline.
It isn't a lipstick shade.
It's not how gracefully you sip your drink
or how well you cross your legs.
Modernity is **dissent.**
It's speaking when silence
would keep you safe.
It's drawing boundaries in steel,
and saying "No" without an apology.
It's not about being better than men—
It's about not being **less than human.**

Priyanka said—
"Feminism isn't about hating men.
It's about the fact that I have the same rights as you.
I can do whatever I want."
And I carry those words on my spine.
This isn't about imitation.
This isn't about competition.
This is about **autonomy.**
The right to be whole.

And then Acharya Prashant's voice—
thunder through my mind—
"A woman must not be worshipped; she must be understood.
She is not a goddess—she is a person."
Do you hear that?
We don't need pedestals.
We need space.

Because those pedestals—
They're just cages in disguise.
We've been cast as
the perfect daughter,
the sacrificing mother,
the obedient wife,
the tireless coworker.
Angel or witch—
nothing in between.
And the real violence?
It's not in the insults.
It's in the **expectations.**
The quiet theft of our right to be flawed,
to be human.
So here's my rebellion:
I am stepping off the pedestal.
Not in shame—
in freedom.
I will be angry.
I will be messy.
I will be bold.
I will be unsure.
I will grow—
without asking your permission.
Modernity is clarity.
It's the clean edge of truth
cutting through the fog.
It's knowing my courage
might threaten your comfort—
and not caring.

Because maybe—
it's your comfort
that needs questioning.
And I will keep asking:
Who am I beneath all these roles?
Am I living on my own terms—
or on a script that's been
stamped "empowerment"
just to keep me quiet?
Am I dressing for freedom—
or undressing for permission?

This is not rebellion for the sake of noise.
This is rebellion for the sake of **truth.**
So no—
I don't want to be your idea of a "modern woman."
I don't want your applause.
I want space.
I want a choice.
I want the freedom
to fail,
to rise,
to question,
to exist—
without being compared,
without being watched,
without being worshipped.
To every woman listening:
You are **not** marble.
You are **not** carved to please.

You are fired.
You are water.
You are the voice.
You are breathing.
You are not here to fit.
You are here—
to **be.**
With truth.
And with thunder.

11. When I Am Silent

The tremor in my bones
could bring down everything I've built.

So when I go quiet,
let me stay there—

until the cyclone
spends itself,
until the storm in my chest
runs out of wind,
until the sea inside me
stops tearing at its own shores.

Silence is not absence.
It is the rope I cling to
while the dark water
tries to pull me under.

12. No Home

No longer does home hold its familiar embrace,
Each corner feels foreign, a desolate space.
We drift like lost shadows, unclaimed and alone,
In a world where connection has turned into stone.
Though it may sound poetic, it cuts like a knife,
These murky reflections reveal a lost life.
In the depths of my mind, I wander through night,
A labyrinth of questions, devoid of all light.
Who am I now? What have I turned into?
With no place to anchor, no soul to hold true.
Irony whispers that solitude's sweet,
For sharing our thoughts often leads to defeat.
We tire of the struggle, the pain of the wait,
Longing for solace, our true home, our fate.
An eternal abode where our spirits can soar,
A sanctuary waiting, forever and more.

13. Not A Complaint But A Hope

Lately, I have felt a soft and steady drift—
not the kind that comes from lack of care,
but the kind born from caring so deeply
that it aches.

When I miss you,
it doesn't always come out as longing.
Sometimes it's sharper,
sometimes it's a little storm
over something small—
a word, a glance, a moment.
It's not anger.
It's just me saying,
"I need you here."

Your time,
your presence,
your warmth—
they matter to me more than I can shape into the right words.
And maybe I don't always show it the way you would want,
but my love is there,
restless and reaching.

I'm not trying to cause fractures between us.
I want us to be more than a pair of names

linked together in the air.
I want us to be the kind of *together*
that feels like shared breath,
like shoulders leaning toward each other
even in silence.

Yes, there's a fear in me—
a fear born of old wounds,
of the ways I have been hurt before.
And when your voice grows guarded,
or your heart pulls inward,
that fear becomes louder.
It tells me to protect myself.
It tells me to question.

But I don't want walls between us.
I don't want distance to grow moss in the quiet.
I want us to speak through the hard things,
to stand on the same side,
even when the world is against us.

I'm not asking you
to fix every crack in my heart,
nor to be perfect in every moment.
I'm only asking for your open hand,
your willing ear,
your steady presence beside me—
so we face the day as a team,
not as two souls pulling in opposite tides.

I care for you.
I care for us.
And I hope you read this
not as a wound opening,
but as a garden being planted—
a hope for more connection,
more understanding,
more ***us.***

14. Unheard Pleas

I witness souls descending,
Shattered, weeping, bleeding,
Voices trapped in silence,
Yet smiles are still misleading.
They yearn to speak their truths,
But words remain unspoken,
Regret for love once cherished,
Now a bond forever broken.
Fate plays its cruel hand,
What circles back will sting,
Once hearts are torn asunder,
They cannot mend or cling.
No love can linger long,
When trust has turned to dust,
Sweet apologies may echo,
Yet healing's not a must.
Injustice wears a mask,
And time can be unkind,
Treasure what you hold dear,
Or leave it all behind.
For hearts are twisted vessels,
Forgiveness may reside,
But memories unforgotten,
Will haunt you deep inside.
Your words, your careless actions,
Have left their bitter mark,

So cherish fragile feelings,
Don't snuff out love's bright spark.
For those who drift away,
Rarely find their way back home,
So guard your heart with kindness,
And never let it roam.

15. A New Path Together

When I stand beneath the sun with you,
Our shadows dance, a gentle hue,
I cherish every moment, every glance,
Where I stood proud, embraced by chance.
I wish to stay just as I am,
When it comes to you, my heart's own jam.
With your hand in mine, we'll forge ahead,
On paths familiar and those unsaid.

Though fear may whisper, and doubt may creep,
I long for shadows that softly sweep,
While sunlight bathes us in its warm embrace,
Uniting our souls in this sacred space.
For in my heart, a dream takes flight,
Yet love's sweet promise feels out of sight.
But still, our bond, like stars, will gleam,
As shadows fade, we'll chase the dream.

Together we'll rise, our faces aglow,
To greet a new dawn, where love can flow.
So let the past linger far behind,
For in this moment, our hearts entwined.

16. Elegy For The Living And The Lot Lost

All things, it seems, converge upon a single soul— a universe folded into one fragile frame.
And when that frame breaks, it leaves behind an unfillable hollow where dreams once breathed.

In a moment, the one you cherished lies still beneath the soil, wrapped in shrouds, or vanishes in fire, or hangs suspended in the air between agony and release. Some simply fade— a slow unraveling into silence.

The world speaks of them, but does not know them.
Judgments bloom like weeds over untended graves, while the truth of their hearts remains unseen.

We walk among each other now as soldiers in an unseen war, each sunrise another battle for survival. Perhaps our humanity slipped away, grain by grain, into the dark. Or perhaps, and this is the crueler thought— we were never human at all.

PROTECTION = CONTROL
HONOR = POLICE
Scripture
The Gentleman's Cage

17. The Gentleman's Cage

They say men have always respected women,
but only when the rulebook allowed it—
when patriarchy painted halos
on the heads of wives who stayed silent,
mothers who fed everyone but themselves,
daughters who never learned the taste of defiance.

Respect, you see,
was never a birthright for her—
it was a reward system,
earned by obedience,
paid in submission.

In houses where the father's word
was scripture carved in stone,
and the mother's dreams
were folded away with winter clothes,
boys grew into kings
who believed a crown was their birthmark.

They learned that "protection"
was just a prettier word for control.
That "honor" meant policing a woman's laugh,
her skirt, her friends, her hours.
That love could be measured
in the thickness of walls

and the number of locked doors.

And so they guarded her—
the way a jailer guards his prisoner.
With watchful eyes,
with iron keys,
with the arrogance of ownership.

Morality?
It exists only in wedding speeches
and school textbooks,
gilded and untouchable.
Reality is raw and rotting—
a truth that crawls,
that snarls,
that bites deeper than hunger.

The wildest beast kills for survival.
Man kills for ego.
And still calls it tradition.

Generations pass.
The leash changes color,
the cage grows velvet bars,
but the rules stay the same—
you may live, breathe,
eat, and sleep,
but only because a man allows it.

And yet—

he stands before the mirror,
chest out, voice firm,
and calls himself
a ***gentleman.***

18. Love Letter

In the shadows of my heart, I tremble,
For the ink quivers, hesitant to flow,
I am afraid to pen a love letter to you,
For you are a vision, a fleeting dream,
A whisper of hope that may vanish at dawn,
I am afraid to weave my words into a tapestry,
For I wonder if your heart beats in rhythm with mine,
I am afraid to inscribe my feelings on paper,
For you seem a distant star, a cloud beyond reach,
I am afraid to etch my affection in ink,
For your essence feels sacred, untouched,
And I fear my words may tarnish your light,
I am afraid to pour my soul onto the page,
For I carry the weight of a heart once shattered,
I am afraid to unveil my wounds to you,
For I have wept crimson tears in silence,
I am afraid to offer my heart, so fragile,
For I doubt I can mend the chasm within you,
I am afraid to speak my truth beneath the stars,
For I do not see your gaze searching for me,
I am afraid to declare my love so pure,
For you seem a miracle, too wondrous to grasp,
I am afraid to write this letter, this plea,
Yet, will you take my trembling hand,
And guide me through this labyrinth of fear?

19. Lost Tales

As I tread the paths of yesteryear,
I stumble on dreams that disappear,
Trust once held, now lies in dust,
Desires unquenched, in shadows rust.
In love's cruel game, betrayal's sting,
I glimpse the ghost of what I bring.
A self entombed, in sorrow's shroud,
With hatred's scent, I stand unbowed.

Wounds and bruises, a tale of time,
Each scar is a verse, a silent rhyme.
I see the chains that bind my soul,
Yearning to rise, yet losing control.
But hope has fled, and passion wanes,
In the echo of loss, only pain remains.
For now I know, it’s not my heart,
But others' views tear apart.

All things must fade, as shadows blend,
And I, once more, shall meet my end.

20. Dreams In The Moor

I long to wander the moors,
Beneath the moon's soft, silver glow,
To hear the brook's enchanting tune,
And revel in the nightingale's flow.
In the hush of the midnight hour,
I yearn to see the ancient gulmohar,
Standing proud in fields of tulips bright,
Inhaling your fragrance, a sweet memoir.
I wish to gaze into your eyes,
In timeless moments, forever entwined,
To kiss your lips, to hold your hand,
And feel the rhythm of your heart aligned.
This is my dream, my heart's desire,
To walk beside you, through life's endless fire,
Until the stars fade and the world departs,
Together, forever, bound by our hearts.

21. His Tales

In the quiet moments, I found a change,
A transformation, subtle yet profound,
Listening became a cherished art,
For him, the one whose laughter knows no bounds.

His voice, a gentle breeze that stirs the soul,
Eyes sparkling with tales of innocence and light,
Each word he weaves, a tapestry of delight,
Turning mundane whispers into stories whole.

With every anecdote, he paints the air,
From childhood dreams to secrets softly shared,
A symphony of thoughts, a dance of care,
In his presence, I find my heart laid bare.

I lean in close, offering my soft replies,
A chorus of "haan" and "hmm" that flows,
He shines, the star of this intimate reprise,
As I bask in the warmth of the love he shows.

He teaches me to embrace the quiet grace,
To me silence blooms, and new joys are born.

From gully tales to the grind of daily strife,
Each story unfolds like a melody sweet,
In his laughter, I find the rhythm of life,

A reminder that beauty in simplicity meets.

Perhaps it's him who brings forth this delight,
Transforming the ordinary into the divine,
In his presence, the world feels just right,
As we share our hearts, our souls intertwine.

Relics of Your Memory
Only by the Just

22. Relics Of Your Memory

In shadows deep, I find your trace,
A longing fierce, a tender grace.
Your absence strikes like winter's chill,
A piercing ache, a void to fill.
I yearn to whisper, "It's not the end,"
For in my heart, you still transcend.
I linger here, a faithful ghost,
Awaiting you, my cherished host.
Your laughter dances like the dawn,
A radiant sun, forever drawn.
Those eyes, a sea of love profound,
In their embrace, my solace was found.
An angel's face, so pure, divine,
Your heartbeat plays a sweet design.
Together, we could brave the tide,
No tempest could turn the ride.
I long to clasp your hand once more,
With warmth that echoes from before.
You dwell within, a sacred tome,
A letter penned, a love's true home.
My heart, a garden, where you reside,
Like secret blooms, where dreams abide.
In hidden realms, our love shall stay,
As Isabella kept her love at bay.
The world may turn, and time may fade,

Yet in my soul, your light is laid.
Though you have gone, like autumn's breath,
You took a piece, yet love knows no death.
I cradle you, a relic rare,
In whispered prayers, a silent prayer.
Forever held, in sacred trust,
To be seen only by the just.

23. Now That You're Mine

O, thou art a specter in my dreams,
Though never have we walked the same path,
Yet in the vast expanse of our shared skies,
We linger like stars, twinkling in the dark,
Each whisper of the wind a call to thee,
A tale spun from joy and sorrow alike,
In the tapestry of fate, we are not mere strangers,
For thou art neither my lord nor I thy lady,
Yet our souls entwined, like silken threads,
Woven in a cocoon of serendipity,
A chance encounter, rare as the moon's embrace.
Once, thou didst stray from the course of my heart,
Yet not for a heartbeat were we apart,
For thou didst cradle my essence through time,
As our affection blossomed, transcending the sublime.

Now, as our fates converge, as lovers destined,
I shall enshrine thee within my heart's sacred chamber,
And thou, in turn, shall hold me, a cherished flame,
In the eternal dance of love, we shall remain.

24. A Soul Reborn

In the embrace of sun and moon's soft glow,
The whispering winds and rivers flow,
Where brooks do babble and blossoms fall,
In the dance of rain, I heed their call.

Life and death, in a tender waltz,
Joy and sorrow, in their vaults,
Mirth and madness, a fleeting thread,
In the tapestry of all that’s said.

To bleed and heal, a cycle spun,
In solitude's grasp or company won,
The silence sings a symphony sweet,
Where kindness and ruthlessness oft do meet.

In flailing doubts or decisions made,
Trust may falter, yet hope won’t fade,
Surprises linger, while knowing stays,
All these currents weave my days.

Through me they pass, a ceaseless stream,
Transforming my essence, like a waking dream,
Into a visage, rare and unseen,
A soul reborn, in twilight's sheen.

GUILT

25. The Thing That Dwells Within

It came to me not as beast nor man,
But as a hush—cold, deliberate, and wan;
A whisper stitched in the air's black seam,
Slipping between the ribs like a fevered dream.

Its breath was mildew, grave-cold and deep,
It coiled in my marrow, it gnawed in my sleep;
Its eyes were voids where no stars dwell,
And in their gaze, I heard the knell.

It drank of my joy, drop by trembling drop,
Till the world grew pale and the clocks did stop;
Even the sun became a ghostly hue,
And shadows spoke in voices few.

Guilt became its scripture, carved in bone,
In letters no mortal hand had known;
It read to me of my smallest sins,
Till I felt my flesh grow thin.

Once, I tried to flee into light's embrace—
Yet the Thing had followed, without a face;
Its hand was the night, its fingers the cold,
It clutched my heart in a grip of old.

Now I walk as a guest in my own skin,

My soul but a candle that gutters within;
And at the mirror, where my eyes should be—
It stares.
It smiles.
It waits for me.

26. Shadow Of The Past

In the depths of my weary soul, I yearn to cast aside the shadows of my past,
To erase the echoes of a life where I have bled,
Where tears have carved rivers upon my cheeks,
And the weight of mourning has draped itself upon my shoulders.
Through the trials, I have learned to rise,
To stand resilient against the storms that life has unleashed.
Yet now, I long for the gentle embrace of your solace,
To surrender myself to the sanctuary of your arms,
Where safety wraps around me like a tender cocoon.
I crave the warmth of your presence,
A balm for the wounds that still linger in the corners of my heart.
Let me weep freely, unburdened by the scars of yesterday,
And in your love, I seek the promise of healing.
Will you be the light that chases away my darkness?
Will you cradle my spirit with the affection it so desperately seeks?
Will you be the radiant sun that brightens my world anew?

27. In That Gentle Moment

In a distant morrow, perchance I shall bestow a smile upon the shadows of yore,
In that fleeting hour, my anguish may wane, like the tide retreating from the shore.
In a time yet to dawn, I may unearth the joy that eludes my weary soul,
In that gentle moment, my heart may dance, as the winds of fate take their toll.

In a future bright, I may discover a love, tender and true,
In that sacred space, perhaps a kindred spirit shall seek me anew.
In the embrace of spring's sweet breath, I may awaken to life's gentle song,
In that cherished season, I shall rise from the scars that have lingered too long.

In the depths of my being, I may come to know I am worthy of bliss,
In that revelatory instant, I shall find you, the essence of my heart's wish.
In the realm of dreams, I may weave visions of a future yet to unfold,
In that enchanted twilight, I shall clasp your hands, as our destinies are told.

In the warmth of your gaze, I may feel the melting of my guarded heart,
In that tender glance, the rain shall transform, a symphony of joy to impart.
In the embrace of summer's eve, hope shall greet me with a gentle sigh,
In that luminous moment, no force shall sever the bond that we tie.

In the twilight of our years, we may stroll hand in hand, side by side,
In that sacred journey, I may find solace, in love's eternal tide.
In the final breath of life, perhaps I shall find peace in your embrace,
In that ultimate surrender, I shall rest, forever in your grace.

Whispers before the dark
Only kindness stays behind— And even that fades with time.

28. Whispers Before The Dark

Verse 1

The tighter I hold, the more it slips—
Time through my fingers, dust on my lips.
The faces I love, the hands I know,
Drift from my reach, and still I let go.

Verse 2

Nothing holds, nothing stays,
The night swallows even the brightest days.
I walk with the thought, the truth I've found—
All that we keep will sink to the ground.

Refrain

In the end, we say goodbye.
Beneath the earth, beneath the sky.
Only kindness stays behind—
The rest is lost to the turning mind.

Verse 3

One day I'll fade, and they will remain,
Living their lives, forgetting my name.
A whisper in wind, a shadow in rain,
Gone with the years, yet still the same.

Refrain

In the end, we say goodbye.
Beneath the earth, beneath the sky.
Only kindness stays behind—
The rest is lost to the turning mind.

Verse 4

So I walk this road, quiet and slow,
Giving what light I still can bestow.
For when I am gone, and they carry on,
Kindness will echo when I'm withdrawn.

Final Refrain

In the end, we say goodbye.
Beneath the earth, beneath the sky.
Only kindness stays behind—
And even that fades with time.

If I brought you a Gulmohor

29. If I Brought You A Gulmohar

One winter's eve, as the wind gnawed at the shutters,
the thought returned—
if I brought you Gulmohar blooms,
scarlet as the blood that once warmed me,
and laid them at the foot of your bed,
would you wake… and smile?

Would you press them between the frail, yellowed pages
of your ancient books,
where the ink is blurred by decades of breath,
and let their hue seep
into the unfinished lines where we last met—
that night when the candle died too soon?

Or would you hide them in the secret drawer
of your blackened oak desk,
beneath the shroud of a white handkerchief,
where only the dead
are permitted entry?

Would you carry them down to the riverbank,
where the water runs slow and glassy,
and, under the shivering moon,
write a new poem in the frost,
where I wander silent and unseen
between your words?

Or would you slip them beneath your pillow,
in the bed where you lie alone,
and dream of a heartbeat
you have not felt for years—
yet feel it still,
pressing from the other side?

But then I recall—
you never loved flowers,
nor the tokens I gave you…
perhaps not even me.

And yet these thoughts haunt me still—
like the echo of footsteps
on an empty stair—
leading, at every turn,
only to the locked room
where I linger,
waiting.

-

The Bride Who Walks the Halls

30. The Bride Who Walks the Halls

I

Beneath the weeping willows' shade,
Where moonlight pales to bone,
A lady walks in bridal lace,
Though centuries have flown.
Her veil is damp with winter rain,
Her eyes a silver gleam,
And all who meet her silent gaze
Are taken to her dream.

II

They say her heart was shattered once,
By love turned cruel and cold,
And in that wound the shadows crept,
And claimed what they could hold.
Her lips still hold a crimson smile,
Her hands a ghost's caress,
But oh—she walks for vengeance now,
And not for tenderness.

III

She drifts through corridors of dust,
Where candles drown in gloom,

Her footsteps soft as whispered vows
Once spoken in this room.
The music of her rustling gown
Can lure the bravest near,
Until they feel her breath like frost
Against their waiting ear.

IV

For time does not unmake the wound,
Nor cleanse the crimson stain—
It only gives her endless nights
To walk, to love, to drain.
She drinks the warmth of living hearts,
The light from mortal eyes,
And in her kiss, she binds the soul
To halls where no one dies.

V

And so the house stands ever still,
Its windows black with grief,
Its garden choked with roses dark,
Their thorns without a leaf.
But when the wind is sharp with rain,
And bells toll midnight's call,
The lady walks in bridal lace—
And waits for you… to fall.

About Poet Rabiya Nizam

Rabiya, is an educator, freelance content writer, and creative writer, weaves words into a kaleidoscope of emotions and reflections. Hailing from Munger, Bihar, she draws inspiration from everyday life, human connections, and the unspoken depths of feelings. Through her poetry and prose, she aspires not only to tell stories but also to create social impact and bring meaningful change. With a strong passion for social work, Rabiya believes in using the power of writing as a voice for the unheard and as a tool for transformation.

You can connect with her on LinkedIn-
https://www.linkedin.com/in/rabiya-nizam-0b61491ab

Social Awareness About Rare Diseases

What Are Rare Diseases?

Ans. The diseases that have lower prevalence in the population are called rare diseases. They may be found in one in thousands to one in millions. About 95% of the rare diseases do not have any treatment available and only 5% have any treatment. The cost of treatment of these diseases is very high making it impossible for a normal family to afford it. Even the diagnosis of these diseases is difficult and takes approximately 5-6 years to identify right disease.

What Is Hemophilia?

Hemophilia is a rare congenital bleeding disorder in which the patient suffers from prolonged bleeding due to extremely low level or no production of blood clotting factor in their body. In severe hemophilia patients even suffer from spontaneous bleeds into their joints, muscles, tissues or vital body organs that may lead to disability or death if not treated on time. Most of the cases the hemophiliacs become permanent disable due to lack of treatment and rehabilitation post bleeding into their joints or muscles. The treatment is costly factor injection that is transfused intra venous to them. Two common types of Hemophilia are Hemophilia A due to lack of factor 8 and Hemophilia due to lack of factor 9.

The prevalence of hemophilia is around 1 male in every 5000 males for Hemophilia A and 1 male in every 8000 males for Hemophilia B. There are 67% cases with hereditary history in the family but staggering 33% cases are first time with no previous family history. The males are patients and females are carrier of the disease. But in severe cases even the females start to show the symptoms with bleeding and blue patches.

For treatment of Hemophilia A medicine named anti-hemophilia factor 8 or just factor 8 injection is given. For treating Hemophilia B medicine factor 9 injection is given. The dosage is dependent on the type of bleed, severity of bleed, site of bleed and the weight of the person to help raise the factor level in the body.

The most common symptoms include non-stop bleeding of the cut, spontaneous bleed from the gums, bleeding in the urine, bleeding from the nose, bleeding in the GI tract without being hurt, bleeding and swelling in the joints or muscles. You can also see black or dark blue spots or patches on the body which may pain on touching at any stage of life. These patches are very common in toddler to young age.

About Publisher

The publisher of this book titled "**Where the wind circles back**" Written by Rabiya Nizam is "**Power In Me Foundation.**" As the name suggest it is a Trust that works on sustainable development model. It is established to work for the welfare of the people with rare diseases and their families. Publishing is one of the activities to help raise funds to carry out the activities aimed to creating awareness about various rare diseases, provide scholarships for studies, to provide for livelihood training, to provide for healthcare training, to establish centers for their care and various other objectives for social causes.

The authors associated with us follow the same vision to make the society a better place through their creative writing. We encourage raw talents with time-to-time guidance and exposure through our creative platform Ruh-E-Mohabbat by supporting and promoting them.

For any query on our publishing services, or supporting our cause to create awareness about rare diseases while empowering them you can reach us at mpowerinme@ gmail.com. You can even call/whatsapp at +91-8851537816. Website: www.powerinme.org/ www.ruhemohabbat.com

www.ingramcontent.com/pod-product-compliance
Ingram Content Group UK Ltd.
Pitfield, Milton Keynes, MK11 3LW, UK
UKHW021342190726
13845UKWH00027B/686

9 789394 749382